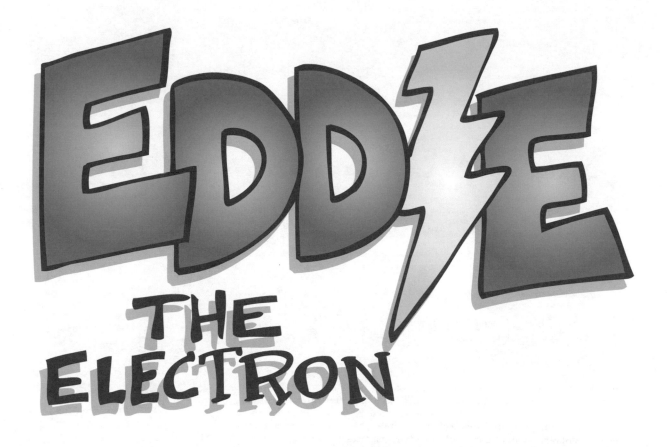

EDDIE
THE ELECTRON

Melissa Rooney

illustrated by Harry Pulver

AMBERJACK
PUBLISHING

Chicago

AMBERJACK
P U B L I S H I N G

Chicago

An imprint of Chicago Review Press Incorporated
814 North Franklin Street
Chicago, Illinois 60610
ISBN 978-0-69246-743-5

 Publisher's Cataloging-in-Publication data

Rooney, Melissa.

    Eddie the Electron / Melissa Rooney ; illustrated by Harry Pulver.
    pages cm
    ISBN 978-0-692-46743-5
    Summary : Eddie the Electron introduces children to basic concepts of atoms, protons and electrons.

1. Electrons --Juvenile literature. I. Pulver, Harry. II. Title.

QC793.5.E62
[539.7/2112] –dc23   2015944461

Published by
AMBERJACK PUBLISHING
An imprint of Chicago Review Press Incorporated
814 North Franklin Street
Chicago, Illinois 60610

Printed in the United States of America

Reviews for *Eddie the Electron*

"*Eddie the Electron* is a fun scientific exploration. Compelling images and engaging language take children on an atomic adventure...This book is a great addition to any classroom."
-Charlotte Peck,
Montessori Primary Teacher

"*Eddie the Electron* bounces with gusto from sub-atomic particles to planets, delivering core scientific concepts in a playful language. Lively illustrations help bring students along for the ride."
-Danielle Quattry Comer,
STEM Teacher
Mother of 2 preschool children

"How many children can be engaged with science because of a single publication? Melissa Rooney's achievement in creating *Eddie the Electron* is explaining the complexities of electrochemistry to the elementary mind in a delightful tale of a Noble atomic particle."
-John Hale,
Co-owner of Binding Time,
Martinsville/Danville, VA

"*Eddie the Electron* is a great instructional resource for helping science come alive for young readers. It is a nice integration of science and literacy. It is a book that is appropriate for the school library, regular classroom, or your own child's bookshelf."
-Elizabeth Ragland,
5th-Grade Social Studies and English

"I bought the book with my 9 year old in mind, and I wasn't too sure my 5 year old would understand much. Boy was I wrong! My 5 year old LOVES the book and asks for it every night at bedtime so he can laugh out loud at the funny illustrations and cheer for Eddie to escape from Erwin, his boring orbit-mate. Meanwhile, my 9 year old impressed her teacher with her knowledge of electrons and protons, all after only one reading of the story. I would most definitely recommend this book to anyone with kids that like funny stories (and whose kids don't?)."

-Paige England Santmyer, parent

"This book is a fabulous introduction to science for kids. My boys, aged 10 and 8, loved it and afterwards talked for a long while about all the things they could imagine if they were an atom!! I agree with Melissa Rooney, the author—we often underestimate how much our children can understand and will be interested in. This book gives them that chance."
-Helen Canny, parent

"This humorous and educational diversion into the social lives of electrons was quite a hit with my 3 and 6 year olds! And I bet it sticks with them a lot longer than most science lessons. Way to make learning some difficult concepts simple and fun!"
-Jennifer Payne Bauer, parent

Hi! My name is Eddie!

Bet you haven't seen an electron like me before! Pretty cute, huh?

I'm round like the perfect bouncy ball.

At least that's how humans like you see me.

Maybe I am a bouncy ball!

But if I am, then I'm one of the super-est of super bouncy balls. I mean, I can fly at the speed of light, man. That's 670 million miles per hour.

That's faster than a race car, a train, or even an airplane! Shoot, even rockets only go about 6,000 miles per hour. They got nothing on me!

In fact, sometimes I go so fast that I make light. That's called fluorescence. You'll learn all about it in high-school chemistry class.

PERIOD

GRAIN
OF SAND

Let's see...where was I?

If I am a bouncy ball, I'd also have to be the smallest one in the world. I mean, you can't even see me with a microscope, dude. At least not the kind they have in your typical science museum.

SPECK
OF
DUST

EDDIE

Anyway, I'm really, REALLY small.

Smaller than the period at the end of this sentence.

Smaller than the smallest particle of dust.

I am a planet in a tiny solar system. Like your earth, I revolve around a sun — well, a big packet of protons, actually. And my whole solar system fits in a space about 3 billion times smaller than the tip of a pencil.

Yeah! There are 3 billion little solar systems on the tip of your pencil. Hard to believe, I know. But it's true. Just ask your mom and dad.

Anyhoo. Here's the deal.
I'm an electron on a helium atom.
You know, the gas that makes birthday balloons
float up in the air? Well, one of these balloons has, like,
a quadrillion helium atoms in it.

And I'm on one of these helium atoms. In fact, I'm
one of only two electrons on my helium atom. Since
my nucleus has only two protons, it can only have two
electrons.

And that's me and Erwin over there.

Hi Erwin!

Erwin doesn't talk. He doesn't even smile. I don't even know his real name —I just call him Erwin because...

Well, because he kind of looks like an Erwin, doesn't he?

He's gotta be the most boring electron in the universe.

You'd think he would be the perfect orbit-mate. I mean, it's like he's not even here, right?

In essence, I have this whole nucleus all to myself.

Even if it only has two protons, it's still a pretty big place for a little electron like me—me and Erwin, that is. Lots of room to move around. And with Erwin being as indifferent as he is, I have lots of privacy and alone time. So what could my problem be, you may ask?

Well, what do you think?

What do you mean, you don't know?

How would you like to live your whole life all by yourself?

Uh, with blank-faced Erwin here.

Erwin!

Hellooooo Erwin!

Nothing. Not even a blink.

The only time I ever even SEE another electron is when my helium atom bumps into another helium atom, and then it's too fast to do anything but wave hello as we fly by one another.

To put it plainly, I'm lonely.

So I've been thinking up this plan, see? How about you pop a hole in this balloon and let me out of here? I'll still be on this helium atom with Erwin, but I won't be stuck in this balloon.

And there are over a hundred other kinds of atoms out there. The air all around you has bazillions of atoms flying around, like Nitrogen and Oxygen, which you breathe to stay alive. Well, if I can ram into one of those babies, then maybe, just maybe, I could jump off this helium atom, attach myself to another nucleus, and finally get to hang out with another electron, maybe one with a little more personality.

What do you say?

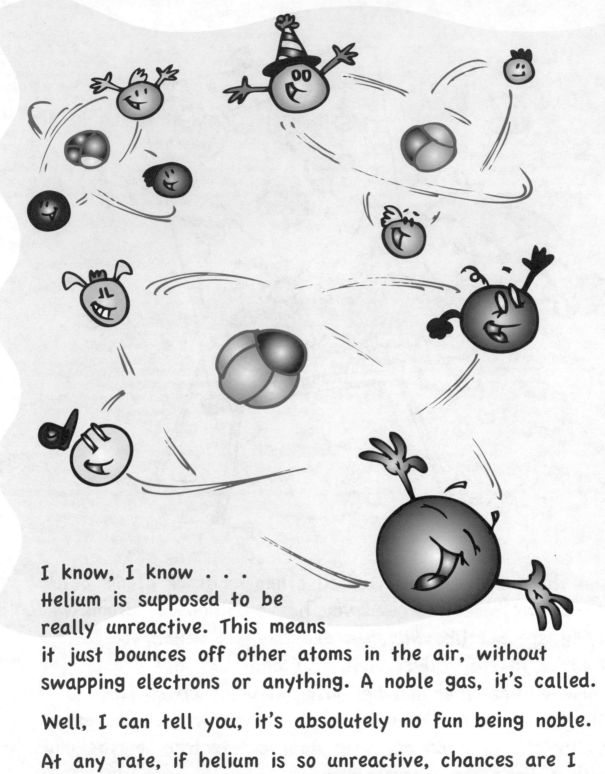

I know, I know . . .
Helium is supposed to be
really unreactive. This means
it just bounces off other atoms in the air, without
swapping electrons or anything. A noble gas, it's called.

Well, I can tell you, it's absolutely no fun being noble.

At any rate, if helium is so unreactive, chances are I
could be stuck on this atom forever, no matter how
many other atoms I ram into.

But even if I never get to another nucleus—even if I'm stuck with Erwin—at least I'll get to see something besides the inside of this balloon.

Chartreuse. Yuck! My least favorite color.

So what do you say?

Can you help me?

Come on...

Just grab some scissors and poke this balloon 'till it pops, and...

What do you mean you aren't allowed to use scissors?!

Just grab this balloon and squeeze it as hard as you can. As HARD as you can.

Until it pops, okay?

No, it shouldn't hurt.

Just keep it away from your face.

There you go.
Hold it down.
Squeeze it.
Squeeze it . . .
Oh I can feel it getting hotter in here.

Yup, you got a good grip, kid!
I must have bumped into 10 billion helium atoms that last second.
Keep squeezing, kid!

Oh yeah, it's getting crowded in here.

Man are we going fast!

Hi, friend!

This sure puts your bumper cars to shame! Woo-hoo!

We're gonna blow!

10, 9, 8, 7, 6, 5, 4, 3, 2, 1—

21

Sorry about the balloon, mate!
Thanks for helping me escape!

See you around!

Get it? Around?

I crack myself up!

MELISSA ROONEY grew up in Martinsville, VA, graduating from Martinsville High School in 1988. After receiving undergraduate degrees in English and Chemistry from the College of William and Mary in Williamsburg, VA, she attended graduate school at the University of North Carolina in Chapel Hill, where she studied electrochemistry under the direction of R. Mark Wightman and was awarded her Ph.D. in Chemistry in 1998. She then conducted research in the laboratory of Alan M. Bond at Monash University in Melbourne, Australia, where she was awarded a Post-Doctoral Fellowship from the Australian Research Council from 2000-2003. In 2002, she returned to North Carolina to raise her family with her husband, Mike Rooney. Since then, Melissa has written for the Durham News (Raleigh News and Observer) and Highlight's Children's Magazine, among other publications, and has received awards for her adult and children's poetry. Melissa is currently a senior scientific editor with American Journal Experts and a teaching artist in the Durham Arts Council's Creative Arts in Public and Private Schools (CAPS) program. She and her husband happily reside in Durham, NC, with their three children. Learn more about Melissa and her writing at www.MelissaRooneyWriting.com.

HARRY PULVER JR. has worked as a professional illustrator for over 30 years. His clients include Crain's New York Business, The Wall Street Journal, Cargill Inc., Coca Cola, Microsoft, 3M, Sony/Epic Music Group, American Lung Assoc., Minnesota Safety Council, Lifetouch Publishing, Target, General Mills, The National Fire Prevention Assoc., Scholastic Inc., Pizza Hut, Allstate Insurance, Levis 501 Jeans, National Geographic World and The Children's Television Workshop.

He attended St. Olaf College, The Minnesota College of Art and Design, and Pratt Manhattan School of Design. You can see more of his artwork or contact him at www.harrypulver.com.